ACCOUNTING BASICS

A Survival Guide for Students

Tracey J. Niemotko, JD, CPA, CFE

Kendall Hunt
publishing company

Cover image provided by Tracey Niemotko

www.kendallhunt.com
Send all inquiries to:
4050 Westmark Drive
Dubuque, IA 52004-1840

Contents

Topic

1 Categories and Accounts..1

2 Did it Increase or Decrease? 13

3 Debits and Credits: The Language of Accounting 23

4 Comprehensive Problem (From Soup to Nuts):
From Transactions to Financial Statements...................49

5 The Comprehensive Problem Revisited.........................79

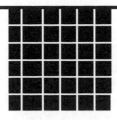

For struggling accounting students everywhere…

Preface

The study of accounting is cumulative. If accounting students do not master basic journal entry preparation from the beginning of their coursework, they are often overwhelmed for the entire semester. Although there are many excellent accounting textbooks, there seems to be a void of supplemental resources available to assist students who are struggling.

It is not uncommon for students to say that they can do well in other courses, but not in accounting. Students are more accustomed to merely memorizing for an exam, and often find the application of the accounting material to be a challenge. Yet understanding accounting can be very rewarding. After all, accounting is the language of business.

In this guide, basic accounting concepts are explained step-by-step, with a focus on accounting for an entrepreneur in a sole proprietorship. In the final unit, a comprehensive problem is presented in order to illustrate the accounting process. Blank accounting paper is provided so that students may complete the problem themselves and review their results.

Professor Niemotko has taught accounting for over thirty years and can identify the obstacles that confront students. *Accounting Basics: A Survival Guide for Students* clarifies and reinforces the fundamental concepts of accounting so that students may feel confident as they progress through their accounting coursework.

Categories and Accounts

Notes

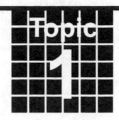

Categories and Accounts

Learning Objectives:

❖ List and define the five basic categories in accounting.
❖ Identify the accounts for each of these categories.

The five basic categories in accounting are as follows:

1. ASSETS
2. LIABILITIES
3. EQUITY
4. REVENUES
5. EXPENSES

According to the language of accounting, a category is the broad grouping of individual accounts. For example, *Cash* is an account under the category **assets**. *Accounts Payable* is an account under the category **liabilities**. *Capital* is an account under the category **equity**, and so on. In this topic, each of the five categories is defined and some examples of specific accounts are presented.

1. ASSETS

Assets are the possessions of a business, or what a business owns and uses. Some accounts under this category are:

> *Cash*
> *Accounts Receivable*
> *Supplies*
> *Computers*
> *Trucks*
> *Vehicles*
> *Equipment*
> *Furniture and Fixtures*
> *Land*
> *Buildings*

Notes

A business may have cash, supplies, computers, trucks or other vehicles, equipment, furniture and fixtures, land, and other assets in order for it to operate. An Accounts Receivable arises when a business sells *on account* or gives credit to a customer and will *receive* payment at a later time.

Where does a business get its assets?

A business may acquire cash and other assets by either:

- Debt financing or
- Equity financing

Debt financing arises when an entrepreneur borrows money for his business from either a bank or some other source, or makes a purchase for the business on credit. Equity financing occurs when the owner or entrepreneur himself contributes the cash or other assets to his business.

Think about it! This applies on a personal level as well. The possessions that an individual owns are financed by either debt or equity. For example, if an individual buys a car, he may pay for it by making a down payment with *his* money (equity financing), regardless of the source, and borrowing the remainder (debt financing).

2. LIABILITIES

Liabilities are the debts or bills of a business—in other words, what a business owes. Generally, accounts under this category end with the word "Payable." Two main accounts are:

- Accounts Payable
- Notes Payable

An *Accounts Payable* arises when a business buys from a supplier on *account* or on credit and will *pay* at a later time. Just like a credit card account, an accounts payable is a line of credit that may be continually charged and repaid. Businesses usually complete a credit application or are approved for credit in order to establish this arrangement. The balance of Accounts Payable increases each time a purchase is made on account because the amount owed increases. Likewise, the balance of Accounts Payable decreases each time a payment is made because the amount owed decreases.

A *Notes Payable* arises when a business borrows money from a bank or some other financial institution. The loan contract that spells out all of the terms of the loan agreement such as the interest rate and the repayment amounts and dates is called the promissory note (or notes payable in accounting).

Unlike an accounts payable that is a revolving line of credit, a business has to reapply for each new loan or notes payable requested. Accordingly, a notes payable is considered a more formal type of loan arrangement.

Notes

3. EQUITY

Equity is an owner's worth or investment in his business. For an entrepreneur who operates his own business, or sole proprietorship, the main account under this category is called the *Capital* account. If Sandy O'Malley is the entrepreneur, then the name of the Capital account is O'Malley, Capital. The Capital account is used like a scorecard to keep a record of the entrepreneur's worth in the business.

Factors that affect the Capital account:

The Capital account increases by:	The Capital account decreases by:
A) Investments **B) Net Income**	**C) Drawings or Withdrawals** **D) Net Loss**

A) Investments

An entrepreneur makes an investment in his business when he contributes cash or other possessions like computers, equipment or land. The balance of the Capital account increases by the amount of the investment made. For example, if an entrepreneur invests cash of $500 in his business, his Capital account increases by $500.

An entrepreneur gets credit for the market value of any non-cash investment that he contributes. For example, an entrepreneur may own land that he originally purchased for $50,000 that has a market value of $100,000. He could sell this land and receive $100,000. If, instead, he gives this land to his business, his Capital account will increase by $100,000--the market value of his investment in his business.

B) Net Income

An entrepreneur's equity in his business increases when profit or net income is earned. Accordingly, the Capital account, which keeps the record of the entrepreneur's equity, increases by net income. For example, an entrepreneur may sell a product for $10 and have expenses totaling $6. His Capital account increases by the net income or profit (ignoring taxes) of $4 (revenues of $10 – expenses of $6).

C) Drawings or Withdrawals

From time to time, an entrepreneur may take money from his business for his own personal living expenditures. Just as an employee is paid a paycheck, the entrepreneur pays himself a "draw" or drawings. When withdrawals are taken, the balance in the owner's Capital account is decreased. For example, if an entrepreneur draws $100 from his business, the balance in his Capital account decreases by $100.

Notes

Drawings decrease an entrepreneur's worth in a business because there is less money invested in the business when it is withdrawn for the personal use of the owner. Although the *owner's* cash increases, the *business'* cash decreases. *The focus in accounting is the viewpoint of the business.*

A separate equity account, Drawings or Withdrawals, may be used instead of the Capital account to record withdrawals. If Drawings is used, it eventually gets closed out and the balance in the account is transferred as a reduction to Capital.

D) Net Loss

Sometimes expenses are greater than the revenues earned. For example, an entrepreneur may sell a product for $10 and have expenses totaling $12. The result would be a $2 net loss (revenues $10 – expenses $12). The entrepreneur must pay the $2 loss himself from the equity in his business; namely, from the cash that he has previously earned or invested.

4. REVENUES

Revenues are the proceeds from selling a product or providing a service to customers. The name of the revenue account may vary, depending upon what is suitable for a particular business. Some revenue accounts are:

> - Sales
> - Fees Earned
> - Service Income
> - Commissions Earned

Sales may be the appropriate name of the revenue account for a business that sells a product. Perhaps *Fees Earned* or *Service Income* may be used for a business that provides a service. *Commissions Earned* may be the name of the revenue account for a realty company, and so on.

5. EXPENSES

Expenses are the costs incurred or generated by a business in order to bring in revenues. For example, a business may have to rent office space and pay for utilities and a telephone in order to conduct business. Further, employees may be hired. Accounts under this category are easy to identify because they end in the word "Expense." Some expense accounts are:

> - Rent Expense
> - Utility Expense
> - Telephone Expense
> - Wages Expense
> - Depreciation Expense

Depreciation is an expense that occurs when the costs of certain assets are deducted or "written off" over the years that the assets are used. Trucks, buildings, equipment, furniture and fixtures, and computers are examples of assets that get depreciated.

Notes

End of Topic Check List:

❖ Can you list and define the five basic categories of accounts?
❖ Can you list some accounts for each category?

Categories	Definition	List of Accounts
1		
2		
3		
4		
5		

❖ What increases the Capital account?
  A)
  B)

❖ What decreases the Capital account?
  C)
  D)

Notes

Did it Increase or Decrease?

Notes

Did it Increase or Decrease?

Learning Objectives:

❖ Identify the accounts that are affected by a business transaction.
❖ Determine if the balances of these accounts increase or decrease.

A fundamental concept in accounting is that the balance of any account in any category may increase or decrease as a result of a business transaction. For example, the Cash account increases when a business receives cash and decreases when cash is paid out.

This concept is important because debits and credits are determined based upon whether an account increases or decreases. The following ten transactions identify the accounts (and their categories) affected by the business transactions and explain why the accounts increase or decrease:

Transaction # 1
The business makes a cash sale to a customer.

Cash (Asset) Increases
Sales (Revenue) Increases

The accounts affected are Cash and Sales. The Cash account increases by the amount of the cash received from the sale. The Sales account increases by the amount of the new sale. New sales increase the balance of the Sales account.

Transaction # 2
The business makes a credit sale (gives credit) to a customer.

Accounts Receivable (Asset) Increases
Sales (Revenue) Increases

The accounts affected are Accounts Receivable and Sales. The Accounts Receivable account increases by the amount that the business will receive from this sale. The Sales account increases by the amount of the new sale.

It is important to note that there are two methods of accounting—the *cash basis* and the *accrual basis*. There are criteria to determine which of the two methods may be used by a business. If

Notes

a business operates under the cash basis, the revenues are recognized when the cash is actually received and the expenses are recognized when the bills are actually paid.

Under the *accrual basis*, which is the focus of this guide, revenues are recognized and recorded when they are *earned* (Accounts Receivable is used) even if cash has not yet been received. Likewise, expenses are recognized and recorded when they are *incurred* (Accounts Payable is used) even if they have not yet been paid.

Transaction # 3
The business purchases supplies with cash.

Supplies (Asset) Increases
Cash (Asset) Decreases

The Supplies and Cash accounts are affected. The Supplies account increases by the amount of the supplies purchased. Cash decreases by the amount paid for the supplies.

Transaction # 4
The business purchases supplies on account (with credit).

Supplies (Asset) Increases
Accounts Payable (Liability) Increases

The Supplies and Accounts Payable accounts are affected. The Supplies account increases by the amount of the supplies purchased. Accounts Payable increases by this new debt or bill that the business will pay at a later time.

Just like a credit card arrangement, an accounts payable increases each time a business buys on account and decreases each time a business makes a payment of the balance owed.

Transaction # 5
The business borrows money from the bank.

Cash (Asset) Increases
Notes Payable (Liability) Increases

The accounts affected are Cash and Notes Payable. The Cash account increases by the amount the business borrows. The Notes Payable account increases by the amount of this new loan. *A new loan increases the debt, or the notes payable, of a business.*

The account, Notes Payable, *not* Accounts Payable is affected because a bank loan is a formal loan obligation in contrast to an accounts payable, a line of credit.

Notes

Transaction # 6
The business repays the bank loan.

Notes Payable (Liability) Decreases
Cash (Asset) Decreases

The Cash and Notes Payable accounts are affected. The Cash account decreases by the amount of cash paid. The Notes Payable account decreases by the amount of the principal or loan balance repaid. *When a loan is repaid, the debt, or notes payable, of a business is reduced.*

Transaction # 7
The entrepreneur invests cash and equipment in his business.

Cash (Asset) Increases
Equipment (Asset) Increases
Capital (Equity) Increases

In this instance, three accounts are affected. Both the Cash and the Equipment accounts increase by the amounts invested by the entrepreneur. The Capital account, the record keeping account for the entrepreneur, increases by the total of the cash and equipment contributed. *The entrepreneur's Capital account increases by investments.*

Transaction # 8
The entrepreneur takes cash from the business for his personal use.

Capital (Equity) Decreases
Cash (Asset) Decreases

The accounts affected are Capital (Drawings may also be used) and Cash. The Capital account decreases by the amount of the withdrawal or draw. The Cash account decreases by the amount of cash paid. *The entrepreneur's Capital account decreases by drawings.*

Transaction # 9
The business receives and pays the telephone bill.

Telephone Expense (Expense) Increases
Cash (Asset) Decreases

Telephone Expense and Cash are the accounts affected. The Telephone Expense account increases by the amount of the telephone services used. This is an additional cost to the business. The Cash account decreases by the amount paid.

Notes

Transaction # 10

The business receives the phone bill and will pay it at a later time.

Telephone Expense (Expense) Increases
Accounts Payable (Liability) Increases

Telephone Expense and Accounts Payable are the accounts affected. The Telephone Expense account increases by the amount of the telephone services used. The Accounts Payable account increases by the amount of this additional bill. Under the accrual method of accounting, expenses are recognized and recorded when they are incurred (Accounts Payable is used) even though cash has not yet been paid.

Note: There is no pattern to be concerned with when analyzing transactions. Some accounts increase while others may also increase or decrease.

End of Topic Check List:

- Do you understand why the accounts in Transactions #1- #10 increase or decrease?

Notes

Debits and Credits: The Language of Accounting

Notes

Debits and Credits:
The Language of Accounting

Learning Objective:

- Determine the debits and credits needed in order to record an entry in the General Journal.

What is a debit and what is a credit?

Debit = Left
Credit = Right

Imagine each account as a scorecard with a left side (column) and a right side (column). Debit means the left side (column) of the account and credit means the right side (column) of the account.

How are transactions recorded?

When a business transaction takes place, it has to be accounted for by the business, or entered "on the books." This first step in the accounting process is accomplished by recording a journal entry, consisting of debits and credits, in the **General Journal**.

The general journal, like a diary, is used to record the details of the events affecting a business, namely, the date that events take place and the accounts and amounts involved. Debit and credit amounts are recorded in the debit and credit columns. The following is an example of a general journal page:

Notes

GENERAL JOURNAL					
Date	Description	Post. Ref.	Debit	Credit

When is an account debited or credited?

In accounting, debit means left and credit means right. There are rules for each category of accounts that determine when an account is debited or credited *based upon whether the account increases or decreases as a result of a business transaction.*

Notes

Debits and Credits for Each of the Five Categories of Accounts:

1. Assets	Rules for Assets	
All asset accounts follow these rules.	**Debit for Increases** Debit an asset account when it *increases*.	**Credit for Decreases** Credit an asset account when it *decreases*.
2. Liabilities	**Rules for Liabilities**	
All liability accounts follow these rules.	**Debit for Decreases** Debit a liability account when it *decreases*.	**Credit for Increases** Credit a liability account when it *increases*.
3. Equity	**Rules for Equity**	
All equity accounts follow these rules.	**Debit for Decreases** Debit an equity account when it *decreases*.	**Credit for Increases** Credit an equity account when it *increases*.
4. Revenues	**Rules for Revenues**	
All revenue accounts follow these rules.	**Debit for Decreases** Debit a revenue account when it *decreases*.	**Credit for Increases** Credit a revenue account when it *increases*.
5. Expenses	**Rules for Expenses**	
All expense accounts follow these rules.	**Debit for Increases** Debit an expense account when it *increases*.	**Credit for Decreases** Credit an expense account when it *decreases*.

Notes

Why do debits increase assets while credits increase liabilities and equity?

Debt and equity are the two sources of financing for a business. Either a business borrows the money that it needs (debt financing) or it receives funding from an owner (equity financing). Accordingly, assets arise from either debt or equity. This is referred to as the **Accounting Equation**, as follows:

$$Assets = Liabilities + Equity$$

In order to reflect the accounting equation, the rules for assets are the opposite of the rules for liabilities and equity. An increase to an asset account is a debit, which comes from the credit or addition of liabilities (debt) or equity.

Revenue and expense accounts are quasi-equity accounts. The owner's Capital account (equity) increases by revenues and decreases by expenses. Accordingly, a credit, which increases equity, increases revenues. Expenses are recorded as debits since debits decrease equity.

Recording a journal entry in the General Journal:

On August 1, John Smith invests $10,000 to begin his business. This transaction affects the business and must, therefore, be entered "on the books." This means that a journal entry, consisting of debits and credits, must be prepared and recorded in the general journal. The steps needed to prepare the journal entry are as follows:

1. **Identify the accounts (and categories) involved.**
   The Cash (Asset) and the Capital (Equity) accounts are affected by this business transaction.

2. **Determine whether the accounts increase or decrease.**
   The Cash account *increases* by $10,000. The Capital account also *increases* by the $10,000 invested by owner Smith.

3. **For the accounts affected, follow the rules for their categories.**

Rules for Assets and Equity
Debit an asset account when it *increases*. Credit an equity account when it *increases*.

Cash is an asset. According to the rules for this category, an asset is debited when it increases. The Cash account increases by $10,000; therefore, debit Cash for $10,000.

Notes

Capital is an equity account. According to the rules for this category, an equity account is credited when it increases. The Capital account increases by $10,000; therefore, credit Capital for $10,000. The journal entry to record this transaction in the General Journal is as follows:

GENERAL JOURNAL

Date		Description	Post. Ref.	Debit	Credit
Aug.	1	Cash		10,000	
		Smith, Capital			10,000
		To record the $10,000 investment by owner Smith.			

Note that the account that is debited (Cash) is recorded first at the margin of the column. The account that is credited (Smith, Capital) is recorded on the next line after skipping some space from the column. By indenting, it makes it easier to see the accounts that are listed as credits.

More than one account may be debited (or credited) as long as the total dollar amount of debits is equal to the total dollar amount of credits ($10,000 total debits = $10,000 total credits). A brief description may be included if useful. The Post. Ref. Column is used to record the ledger account number and is discussed in Topic Four.

Further, it does not matter whether one account or all accounts are increasing or decreasing. *"Increases"* and *"decreases"* are not matched in any way. They are only relevant for determining the debit or credit for each account based upon the rules for the category. Also, in a single transaction, all the accounts may fall under the same category and follow the same rules.

In Topic Two, ten transactions were analyzed to determine whether the accounts increased or decreased. Debits and credits may now be determined for each of these ten transactions, and journal entries may be prepared in the General Journal.

Transaction # 1
The business makes a cash sale to a customer.

Cash (Asset) Increases
Sales (Revenue) Increases

Rules for Assets and Revenues

Debit an asset account when it *increases.*
Credit a revenue account when it *increases.*

According to the rules for assets, an increase to an asset account is recorded as a debit. Debit Cash. According to the rules for revenues, an increase to a revenue account is recorded as a credit. Credit Sales. In the language of accounting:

Debit Cash
Credit Sales

Notes

The journal entry is recorded as follows:

GENERAL JOURNAL					
Date	Description	Post. Ref.	Debit	Credit
Sept. 1	Cash		x	
	Sales			x
	To record the cash sale to a customer.			

(Note: X is used to represent dollar amounts.)

Transaction # 2
The business makes a credit sale (gives credit) to a customer.

Accounts Receivable (Asset) Increases
Sales (Revenue) Increases

Rules for Assets and Revenues

Debit an asset account when it *increases*.
Credit a revenue account when it *increases*.

According to the rules for assets, an increase to an asset account is recorded as a debit. Debit Accounts Receivable. According to the rules for revenues, an increase to a revenue account is recorded as a credit. Credit Sales. In the language of accounting:

Debit Accounts Receivable
Credit Sales

The journal entry is recorded as follows:

GENERAL JOURNAL					
Date	Description	Post. Ref.	Debit	Credit
Sept. 1	Accounts Receivable		x	
	Sales			x
	To record the credit sale to customer Smith.			

Transaction # 3
The business purchases supplies with cash.

Supplies (Asset) Increases
Cash (Asset) Decreases

Notes

Rules for Assets

Debit an asset account when it *increases*.
Credit an asset account when it *decreases*.

According to the rules for assets, an increase to an asset account is recorded as a debit. Debit Supplies. A decrease to an asset account is recorded as a credit. Credit Cash. In the language of accounting:

Debit Supplies
Credit Cash

The journal entry is recorded as follows:

GENERAL JOURNAL

Date		Description	Post. Ref.	Debit	Credit
Sept.	2	Supplies		x	
		Cash			x
		To record the purchase of supplies from ABC Stationers.			

In this transaction, both accounts are categorized as assets. As long as the total debits and credits for the transaction are equal, both accounts may be subject to the rules of the same category.

Transaction # 4
The business purchases supplies on account (with credit).

Supplies (Asset) Increases
Accounts Payable (Liability) Increases

Rules for Assets and Liabilities

Debit an asset account when it *increases*.
Credit a liability account when it *increases*.

According to the rules for assets, an increase to an asset account is recorded as a debit. Debit Supplies. According to the rules for liabilities, an increase to a liability account is recorded as a credit. Credit Accounts Payable. In the language of accounting:

Debit Supplies
Credit Accounts Payable

Notes

The journal entry is recorded as follows:

GENERAL JOURNAL					
Date		Description	Post. Ref.	Debit	Credit
Sept.	5	Supplies		x	
		Accounts Payable			x
		To record the purchase of supplies on account from ABC Stationers.			

Transaction # 5
The business borrows money from the bank.

Cash (Asset) Increases
Notes Payable (Liability) Increases

Rules for Assets and Liabilities

Debit an asset account when it *increases*.
Credit a liability account when it *increases*.

According to the rules for assets, an increase to an asset account is recorded as a debit. Debit Cash. According to the rules for liabilities, an increase to a liability account is recorded as a credit. Credit Notes Payable. In the language of accounting:

Debit Cash
Credit Notes Payable

The journal entry is recorded as follows:

GENERAL JOURNAL					
Date		Description	Post. Ref.	Debit	Credit
Sept.	7	Cash		x	
		Notes Payable			x
		To record the bank loan from Money Bank			

Transaction # 6
The business repays the bank loan.

Notes Payable (Liability) Decreases
Cash (Asset) Decreases

Rules for Liabilities and Assets

Debit a liability account when it *decreases*.
Credit an asset account when it *decreases*.

Notes

According to the rules for liabilities, a decrease to a liability account is recorded as a debit. Debit Notes Payable. According to the rules for assets, a decrease to an asset account is recorded as a credit. Credit Cash. In the language of accounting:

Debit Notes Payable
Credit Cash

The journal entry is recorded as follows:

GENERAL JOURNAL					
Date		Description	Post. Ref.	Debit	Credit
Oct.	5	Notes Payable		x	
		Cash			x
		To record the repayment of principal to Money Bank.			
		Or			
Oct.	5	Notes Payable		x	
		Interest Expense*		x	
		Cash			x
		To record the payment of principal and interest to Money Bank.			
* The Interest Expense account is debited for the portion of the repayment that may include interest. The debit indicates the increase to Interest Expense for the interest paid.					

Transaction # 7
The entrepreneur invests cash and equipment in his business.

Cash (Asset) Increases
Equipment (Asset) Increases
Capital (Equity) Increases

Rules for Assets and Equity
Debit an asset account when it *increases*. Credit an equity account when it *increases*.

According to the rules for assets, an increase to an asset account is recorded as a debit. Debit both Cash and Equipment. According to the rules for equity, an increase to an equity account is recorded as a credit. Credit Capital. In the language of accounting:

Debit Cash
Debit Equipment
Credit Capital

Notes

The journal entry is recorded as follows:

GENERAL JOURNAL

Date		Description	Post. Ref.	Debit	Credit
Oct.	9	Cash		x	
		Equipment		x	
		Capital			x
		To record the owner's investment of cash and equipment in his business.			

Transaction # 8
The entrepreneur takes cash from the business for his personal use.

Capital (Equity) Decreases
Cash (Asset) Decreases

Rules for Equity and Assets

Debit an equity account when it *decreases.*
Credit an asset account when it *decreases.*

According to the rules for equity, a decrease to an equity account is recorded as a debit. Debit Capital. According to the rules for assets, a decrease to an asset account is recorded as a credit. Credit Cash. In the language of accounting:

Debit Capital
Credit Cash

The journal entry is recorded as follows:

GENERAL JOURNAL

Date		Description	Post. Ref.	Debit	Credit
Oct.	21	Capital or Withdrawals		x	
		Cash			x
		To record the draw taken by the owner.			

For this transaction, Withdrawals, another equity account, may be debited instead of the Capital account in order to record the draw. The advantage of using Withdrawals is that it records solely the amount of drawings taken by the entrepreneur.

Notes

Transaction # 9

The business receives and pays the telephone bill.

Telephone Expense (Expense) Increases
Cash (Asset) Decreases

Rules for Expenses and Assets
Debit an expense account when it *increases*. Credit an asset account when it *decreases*.

According to the rules for expenses, an increase to an expense account is recorded as a debit. Debit Telephone Expense. According to the rules for assets, a decrease to an asset account is recorded as a credit. Credit Cash. In the language of accounting:

Debit Telephone Expense
Credit Cash

The journal entry is recorded as follows:

GENERAL JOURNAL					
Date		Description	Post. Ref.	Debit	Credit
Oct.	23	Telephone Expense		x	
		Cash			x
		To record the payment of the telephone bill to Telcom.			

Transaction # 10

The business receives the telephone bill and will pay it at a later time.

Telephone Expense (Expense) Increases
Accounts Payable (Liability) Increases

Rules for Expenses and Liabilities
Debit an expense account when it *increases*. Credit a liability account when it *increases*.

According to the rules for expenses, an increase to an expense account is recorded as a debit. Debit Telephone Expense. According to the rules for liabilities, an increase to a liability account is recorded as a credit. Credit Accounts Payable. In the language of accounting:

Debit Telephone Expense
Credit Accounts Payable

Notes

The journal entry is recorded as follows:

GENERAL JOURNAL

Date		Description	Post. Ref.	Debit	Credit
Oct.	30	Telephone Expense		x	
		Accounts Payable			x
		To record the receipt of the phone bill to be paid at a later time.			

End of Topic Check List:

• What is a debit and what is a credit?

Do you recall:

1. Assets	Rules for Assets
All asset accounts follow these rules.	
2. Liabilities	**Rules for Liabilities**
All liability accounts follow these rules.	
3. Equity	**Rules for Equity**
All equity accounts follow these rules.	
4. Revenues	**Rules for Revenues**
All revenue accounts follow these rules.	
5. Expenses	**Rules for Expenses**
All expense accounts follow these rules.	

Notes

Comprehensive Problem (From Soup to Nuts): From Transactions to Financial Statements

Notes

Comprehensive Problem
(From Soup to Nuts):
From Transactions to Financial Statements

Learning Objectives
- Record the transactions in the general journal.
- Post to the general ledger.
- Prepare the trial balance.
- Record adjusting entries and complete the work sheet.
- Prepare financial statements.

Background to the Comprehensive Problem

Sandy O'Malley began his own consulting business on May 1, Year 1, and had several transactions take place during the month. O'Malley wants to have financial statements prepared in order to review the results of his first month of business.

COMPREHENSIVE PROBLEM

Step #1 Record the transactions in the General Journal

Prepare the journal entries for the following May transactions:

May	Sandy O'Malley:
1	Invests $2,000 to begin his business.
1	Pays $1,500 for a three-month insurance policy.
3	Rents an office and pays $1,000 rent for May.
6	Borrows $4,000 from the bank for his business.
8	Buys supplies on account for $900 from XYZ Supplies.
15	Receives $8,000 for consulting services.
20	Pays $700 of the balance due to XYZ Supplies.
28	Pays $400 for the telephone for May.
28	Pays $300 for utilities for May.
28	Pays wages of $2,000 to employees.

Notes

The accounts to be debited and credited are Cash; Supplies; Prepaid Insurance; Accounts Payable; Notes Payable; O'Malley, Capital; Consulting Fees; Rent Expense; Telephone Expense; Utility Expense; Wages Expense.

GENERAL JOURNAL				Page 1	
Year One Date	Description	Post. Ref.	Debit	Credit	
May 1	Cash	100	2,000		
	O'Malley, Capital	300		2,000	
	To record the investment by the owner.				
1	Prepaid Insurance	102	1,500		
	Cash	100		1,500	
	To record payment of three months of insurance (Policy #216754)				
3	Rent Expense	500	1,000		
	Cash	100		1,000	
	To record the payment of rent for May.				
6	Cash	100	4,000		
	Notes Payable	201		4,000	
	To record the loan from Money Bank.				
8	Supplies	101	900		
	Accounts Payable	200		900	
	To record the purchase on account from XYZ.				
15	Cash	100	8,000		
	Consulting Fees	400		8,000	
	To record consulting services earned.				
20	Accounts Payable	200	700		
	Cash	100		700	
	To record the payment to XYZ				
28	Telephone Expense	501	400		
	Cash	100		400	
	To record the payment of the phone bill for May.				
28	Utility Expense	502	300		
	Cash	100		300	
	To record the payment of the utility bill for May.				
28	Wages Expense	503	2,000		
	Cash	100		2,000	
	To record the payment of wages for the month of May.				

Note: The Post. Ref. (Post Reference) column indicates the account number in the general ledger where the above transactions are "posted" or recorded. The May 1 $2,000 debit to Cash is posted to the cash ledger card #100. The $2000 credit to O'Malley, Capital is posted to account #300, and so on.

Step #2 Post to the General Ledger

After the transactions are recorded in the general journal, they are "posted" to the **General Ledger**. Each account has its own ledger card with an assigned ledger number where debits and credits from the general journal are recorded. All of the individual ledger cards together make up the general ledger. The general journal provides the details of the transactions, and the general ledger shows the debits, credits and balances for each account.

Notes

In this exercise, **asset** accounts are assigned numbers beginning with #100, the **liability** accounts begin with #200, the **equity** accounts begin with #300, and so on. These numbers are recorded in the Post Reference (Post. Ref.) column of the general journal to indicate that the amount from the journal was posted to that ledger card. To leave a trail, the general journal page number is, likewise, recorded in the Post Reference (Post. Ref.) column of the general ledger.

Many entrepreneurs use accounting software instead of a manual accounting system. The software provides a chart of accounts or a list of account numbers to debit or credit in order to record transactions on the computer. The software generates the general journal, the general ledger, a trial balance and financial statements, as needed.

Ledger cards are set up for each account that is recorded in the general journal. All debits and credits to the accounts in the general journal are posted as follows:

Cash		GENERAL LEDGER				#100
Date		Item	Post. Ref.	Debit	Credit	Balance
May	1		GJ1	2,000		
	1		GJ1		1,500	
	3		GJ1		1,000	
	6		GJ1	4,000		
	15		GJ1	8,000		
	20		GJ1		700	
	28		GJ1		400	
	28		GJ1		300	
	28		GJ1		2,000	
		Subtotals		14,000	5,900	8,100 (Dr.)

Note:
- There is a debit balance of $8,100 at the end of the month. One way to get this balance is to total the debits ($14,000) and the credits ($5,900) and get the difference between the two columns ($8,100 = $14,000 - $5,900). This is an $8,100 debit balance because the debit subtotal (14,000) exceeds the credit subtotal (5,900). (Debit is abbreviated Dr. and Credit is abbreviated Cr.)
- In the Post. Ref. Column, GJ1 means that the posting came from general journal page #1, GJ2 would refer to a second page of the general journal, and so on ... This leaves a "trail" to the exact journal page in the event that the details of a transaction are needed.
- Each of these ledger cards represents a separate ledger page.

Notes

Supplies   GENERAL LEDGER   #101

Date		Item	Post. Ref.	Debit	Credit	Balance
May	8		GJ1	900		**900(Dr.)**

Prepaid Insurance   GENERAL LEDGER   #102

Date		Item	Post. Ref.	Debit	Credit	Balance
May	1		GJ1	1,500		**1,500(Dr.)**
		Note: Prepaid Insurance (Asset) and not Insurance Expense is debited because coverage is for a period of time beyond the current month.				

Accounts Payable   GENERAL LEDGER   #200

Date		Item	Post. Ref.	Debit	Credit	Balance
May	8		GJ1		900	
	20		GJ1	700		**200(Cr.)**

Notes Payable   GENERAL LEDGER   #201

Date		Item	Post. Ref.	Debit	Credit	Balance
May	6		GJ1		4,000	**4,000(Cr.)**

O'Malley, Capital   GENERAL LEDGER   #300

Date		Item	Post. Ref.	Debit	Credit	Balance
May	1		GJ1		2,000	**2,000(Cr.)**

Consulting Fees   GENERAL LEDGER   #400

Date		Item	Post. Ref.	Debit	Credit	Balance
May	15		GJ1		8,000	**8,000(Cr.)**

Notes

Rent Expense   GENERAL LEDGER   #500

Date		Item	Post. Ref.	Debit	Credit	Balance
May	3		GJ1	1,000		**1,000(Dr.)**

Telephone Expense   GENERAL LEDGER   #501

Date		Item	Post. Ref.	Debit	Credit	Balance
May	28		GJ1	400		**400(Dr.)**

Utility Expense   GENERAL LEDGER   #502

Date		Item	Post. Ref.	Debit	Credit	Balance
May	28		GJ1	300		**300(Dr.)**

Wages Expense   GENERAL LEDGER   #503

Date		Item	Post. Ref.	Debit	Credit	Balance
May	28		GJ1	2,000		**2,000(Dr.)**

Step #3 Prepare the Trial Balance

A Trial Balance is prepared to confirm that the total debit postings and the total credit postings in the general ledger equal or balance. Since debits and credits recorded in the general journal must equal each other, then the total debits and the total credits posted to the ledger should also equal each other. To prepare a trial balance:

1) List the accounts (in order) from the ledger cards.
2) Record the debit or credit balance from the ledger for each account in the debit or credit column on the trial balance.
3) Check if the trial balance is in balance by totaling the debit and credit columns:

Notes

Trial Balance	Debit	Credit
Cash	$8,100	
Supplies	900	
Prepaid Insurance	1,500	
Accounts Payable		$200
Notes Payable		4,000
O'Malley, Capital		2,000
Consulting Fees		8,000
Rent Expense	1,000	
Telephone Expense	400	
Utility Expense	300	
Wages Expense	2,000	
TOTALS	$14,200	$14,200

Note: This Trial Balance "balances" because the total debits ($14,200) are equal to the total credits ($14,200).

Step #4 Prepare Adjusting Entries

It is important to be sure that all revenues and expenses are recorded before financial statements or tax returns are prepared. If revenues or expenses are omitted then the profit calculation will not be correct. To check if revenues and expenses are accounted for, two adjusting entries for revenues and two adjusting entries for expenses should be considered:

Two Adjusting Entries for Revenues:

❖ **Unrecorded Revenues**
Debit Accounts Receivable (Asset)
Credit Consulting Fees (Revenue)

Under accrual accounting, revenues are recorded *when they are earned* even if the cash will be received at a later time. Accordingly, an entrepreneur should determine what revenues he has earned for services that he has not yet billed or received payment. This adjusting entry is initially recorded on the work sheet and then in the general journal as follows:

GENERAL JOURNAL					
Date		Description	Post. Ref.	Debit	Credit
		Accounts Receivable		x	
		Consulting Fees			x
To record the accrued revenues earned through the end of the accounting period.					

Notes

❖ **Prepaid Revenues**
Debit Prepaid Revenue (Liability)
Credit Consulting Fees (Revenue)

Some businesses receive cash in advance before it is earned. Retailers that sell gift certificates, publishers that sell subscriptions, and professionals like attorneys who receive retainers, are paid cash before it is earned.

When an advance is received, the liability account, *Prepaid Revenue* (or Unearned Revenue), is credited, as opposed to the revenue account. This is because the money may have to be refunded if for some reason it is not earned. For example, a subscriber may decide to cancel a magazine subscription and request a cash refund.

As the revenues are earned, the Prepaid Revenue account must be adjusted. If, for example, the attorney has now performed the services and earned the retainer, the prepayment is transferred from the Prepaid Revenue (liability) account to a revenue account. This adjusting entry is initially recorded on the work sheet and then in the general journal as follows:

GENERAL JOURNAL

Date		Description	Post. Ref.	Debit	Credit
		Prepaid Revenue		x	
		Revenues Earned			x
		To record the portion of the prepaid revenue that is now earned. The Prepaid Revenue account is one of the few liability accounts that does not end with the word "Payable."			

Two Adjusting Entries for Expenses:

❖ **Unrecorded Expenses**
Debit an Expense (Expense)
Credit Accounts Payable (Liability)

Under accrual accounting, expenses are recorded *when they are incurred* even if they have not yet been paid. There are a number of expenses that are incurred during a month that may not get paid within that month. For example, a business may incur telephone or utility expenses for the month of December that may not be paid until January or even February of the following year. The same is true for credit card expenditures. Also, there may be wages that are owed to employees as of the end of December that may get paid as part of the next pay period in January.

In these scenarios, an adjusting entry is required to record the expenses in the period that they are incurred even though they will get paid at a later time. This adjusting entry is initially recorded on the work sheet and then in the general journal as follows:

Notes

GENERAL JOURNAL

Date		Description	Post. Ref.	Debit	Credit
		Telephone Expense		x	
		Utility Expense		x	
		Accounts Payable			x
		To accrue the expenses incurred through the end of the accounting period.			

❖ Prepaid Expenses
Debit an Expense (Expense)
Credit the Prepaid Expense (Asset)

When expenses are prepaid, they are recorded as assets. For example, when a business pays for a six-month insurance policy, Prepaid Insurance (Asset) is debited *not* Insurance Expense. This is because the business may cancel the policy and be entitled to a refund for the portion of the insurance that has not expired. Other prepaid expenses are rent and supplies. Depreciation also falls under this category.

If prepaid expenses have become expenses, an adjustment is needed to transfer the amount no longer prepaid to an expense account. This adjusting entry is initially recorded on the work sheet and then in the general journal as follows:

GENERAL JOURNAL

Date		Description	Post. Ref.	Debit	Credit
		Insurance Expense		x	
		Prepaid Insurance			x
		To record the portion of the prepaid insurance that has now expired.			

In summary, the four adjusting entries are:

I. Unrecorded Revenues	III. Unrecorded Expenses
Accounts Receivable x 　　Revenue　　　　　x	_____ Expense　x 　　Accounts Payable　x
II. Prepaid Revenues	IV. Prepaid Expenses
Prepaid Revenue　　x 　　Revenue　　　　　x	_____ Expense　x 　　Prepaid Expense　　x

Notes

The purpose of the adjusting entries is to be sure that all revenues and expenses are recorded for the accounting period. Accordingly, the two adjusting entries for revenues record additional revenues and the two adjusting entries for expenses record additional expenses.

Step #5 Prepare the Work Sheet

The **Work Sheet** is used to finalize the numbers for financial statement and tax return preparation. Accordingly, on the work sheet, the balances of accounts from the trial balance are adjusted. The first step in preparing the work sheet is to record or copy the trial balance onto the trial balance columns. For Sandy O'Malley, the balances are recorded for the month of May as follows:

Work Sheet

Accounts	Trial Balance		Adjusting Entries		Adjusted Trial Balance		Balance Sheet		Income Statement	
	Debit	Credit	Debit	Credit	Debit	Credit	Debit	Credit	Debit	Credit
Cash	8,100									
Supplies	900									
Prepaid Insurance	1,500									
Accounts Payable		200								
Notes Payable		4,000								
O'Malley, Capital		2,000								
Consulting Fees		8,000								
Rent Expense	1,000									
Telephone Expense	400									
Utility Expense	300									
Wages Expense	2,000									
	14,200	14,200								

Before financial statements can be prepared, the following adjusting entries are needed:

(a)

O'Malley determined that $400 of the $900 of supplies purchased during the month were used:

Debit Supplies Expense (Expense) $400
Credit Supplies (Assets) $400

Supplies Expense increases by the $400 worth of supplies used. Likewise, the asset, Supplies, decreases by $400. After this adjusting entry is recorded on the work sheet, a balance of $500 for Supplies is shown on the adjusted trial balance ($900 purchased - $400 used).

(b)

On May 1, O'Malley paid $1,500 for a three-month insurance policy. As of May 31, one month's worth or $500 of the insurance ($1,500 ÷ 3) has expired:

Debit Insurance Expense (Expense) $500
Credit Prepaid Insurance (Asset) $500

Insurance Expense increases by the $500 of expired insurance. The asset, Prepaid Insurance, decreases by this $500 that is no longer prepaid.

Notes

(c)

O'Malley determined that he has earned $2,000 in consulting fees for May for which he has not yet billed clients:

Debit Accounts Receivable (Asset) $2,000
Credit Consulting Fees (Revenue) $2,000

O'Malley has revenues of $2,000 that must be recorded even though he will receive payment at a later time. Both Accounts Receivable and Consulting Fees increase.

Recording the adjusting entries on the work sheet:

Work Sheet

Accounts	Trial Balance		Adjusting Entries		Adjusted Trial Balance		Balance Sheet		Income Statement	
	Debit	Credit	Debit	Credit	Debit	Credit	Debit	Credit	Debit	Credit
Cash	8,100				8,100					
Supplies	900			(a) 400	500					
Prepaid Insurance	1,500			(b) 500	1,000					
Accounts Payable		200				200				
Notes Payable		4,000				4,000				
O'Malley, Capital		2,000				2,000				
Consulting Fees		8,000		(c) 2,000		10,000				
Rent Expense	1,000				1,000					
Telephone Expense	400				400					
Utility Expense	300				300					
Wages Expense	2,000				2,000					
	14,200	*14,200*								
Supplies Expense			(a) 400		400					
Insurance Expense			(b) 500		500					
Accounts Receivable			(c) 2,000		2,000					
			2,900	*2,900*	*16,200*	*16,200*				

The adjusting entries are recorded on the work sheet and adjust the balances of the affected accounts. For example, Supplies had a debit balance of $900 and an adjusted debit balance of $500 after the $400 credit entry. Prepaid Insurance had a debit balance of $1,500 and an adjusted debit balance of $1,000 after the $500 credit entry. (Debits add to debits, credits add to credits, debits and credits net against each other.) If there are no adjustments to an account, the balance from the trial balance is carried to the adjusted trial balance.

Once the adjusted trial balance is prepared, the work sheet can be completed:

❖ Asset, liability, and equity accounts are presented on the balance sheet.
❖ Revenue and expense accounts are presented on the income statement.

Notes

The Completed Work Sheet

Accounts	Trial Balance Debit	Trial Balance Credit	Adjusting Entries Debit	Adjusting Entries Credit	Adjusted Trial Balance Debit	Adjusted Trial Balance Credit	Balance Sheet Debit	Balance Sheet Credit	Income Statement Debit	Income Statement Credit
Cash	8,100				8,100		8,100			
Supplies	900			(a) 400	500		500			
Prepaid Insurance	1,500			(b) 500	1,000		1,000			
Accounts Payable		200				200		200		
Notes Payable		4,000				4,000		4,000		
O'Malley, Capital		2,000				2,000		2,000		
Consulting Fees		8,000		(c) 2,000		10,000				10,000
Rent Expense	1,000				1,000				1,000	
Telephone Expense	400				400				400	
Utility Expense	300				300				300	
Wages Expense	2,000				2,000				2,000	
	14,200	14,200								
Supplies Expense			(a) 400		400				400	
Insurance Expense			(b) 500		500				500	
Accounts Receivable			(c) 2,000		2,000		2,000			
			2,900	2,900	16,200	16,200	11,600	6,200	4,600	10,000
								5,400	5,400	

The $5,400 represents the profit or the net income for the month of May (revenues of $10,000 – expenses of $4,600). From the completed work sheet, financial statements may be prepared.

Step #6 Prepare the Financial Statements

The four basic financial statements that are prepared on behalf of a business are:

➤ The Income Statement
➤ The Balance Sheet or The Statement of Financial Position
➤ The Statement of Owner's Equity
➤ The Statement of Cash Flows

The Statement of Cash Flows, which accounts for the change in cash for a business, is usually studied at a more intermediate level of accounting. Accordingly, the three primary financial statements for Sandy O'Malley are as follows:

Notes

The Income Statement

The purpose of an income statement is to present the results from the operation of a business over a period of time by showing the revenues and expenses and the calculation of net income or loss. The income statement has a heading that includes the name of the business, the statement, and the time period covered. For the first month of operations, Sandy O'Malley earned $5,400 (ignoring taxes):

O'Malley Pro Consultants
Income Statement
For the Month Ended May 31, Year 1

Consulting Fees		$10,000
Rent Expense	$ 1,000	
Telephone Expense	400	
Utility Expense	300	
Wages Expense	2,000	
Supplies Expense	400	
Insurance Expense	500	
Total Expenses		4,600
Net Income		$5,400

Notes

The Statement of Owner's Equity

The Statement of Owner's Equity is an analysis of the entrepreneur's Capital account. Capital increases by net income and investments and decreases by net loss and drawings. On May 1, O'Malley invested $2,000 in his business but took no draw for the month. He earned $5,400 in May. (The income statement is usually prepared first since the net income is needed in order to prepare this statement.) O'Malley's Capital balance at the end of May is $7,400, as follows:

O'Malley Pro Consultants
Statement of Owner's Equity
For the Month Ended May 31, Year 1

Capital Balance May 1, Year 1		$ 0
Add:		
Net Income	$5,400	
Investments	2,000	
Less:		
Drawings	- 0 -	7,400
Capital Balance May 31, Year 1		$ 7,400

There is no beginning balance in the Capital account as of May 1 because this is a new business. The beginning balance for June 1 will be $7,400, the balance from the end of May.

Notes

The Balance Sheet

The balance sheet, or the statement of financial position, lists the assets of a business in the order of liquidity, and shows where the funding came from to obtain them (debt or equity financing). Of the $11,600 in assets, $4,200 was paid for by debt and $7,400 came from O'Malley's pocket:

Assets = Liabilities + Equity

$$\$11,600 = \$4,200 + \$7,400$$

O'Malley Pro Consultants
Balance Sheet
May 31, Year 1

ASSETS

Cash	$8,100
Accounts Receivable	2,000
Supplies	500
Prepaid Insurance	1,000
Total Assets	**$11,600**

LIABILITIES and EQUITY

Accounts Payable	$ 200
Notes Payable	4,000
Total Liabilities	4,200
Equity: O'Malley, Capital	7,400
Total Liabilities and Equity	**$11,600**

Financial statements are very useful to entrepreneurs. O'Malley can check his profit and see the amount that he has invested in his business. By reviewing the assets, O'Malley can determine how his $7,400 investment has been used. The financial statements provide the financial information needed in order to effectively operate a business.

Notes

The Comprehensive Problem Revisited

Notes

The Comprehensive Problem Revisited

The application of the material is a pertinent part of the learning process in accounting. You are encouraged to complete the Comprehensive Problem from Topic Four on the accounting paper provided.

Prepare the journal entries for the following May transactions:

May   **Sandy O'Malley**
1   Invests $2,000 to begin his business.
1   Pays $1,500 for a three-month insurance policy.
3   Rents an office and pays $1,000 rent for May.
6   Borrows $4,000 from the bank for his business.
8   Buys supplies on account for $900 from XYZ Supplies.
15   Receives $8,000 for consulting services.
20   Pays $700 of the balance due to XYZ Supplies.
28   Pays $400 for the telephone for May.
28   Pays $300 for utilities for May.
28   Pays wages of $2,000 to employees.

Notes

GENERAL JOURNAL				
Date	Description	Post Ref.	Debit	Credit

Notes

Cash   GENERAL LEDGER   #100

Date	Item	Post. Ref.	Debit	Credit	Balance
May					

Supplies   GENERAL LEDGER   #101

Date	Item	Post. Ref.	Debit	Credit	Balance
May					

Prepaid Insurance   GENERAL LEDGER   #102

Date	Item	Post. Ref.	Debit	Credit	Balance
May					

Accounts Payable   GENERAL LEDGER   #200

Date	Item	Post. Ref.	Debit	Credit	Balance
May					

Notes Payable   GENERAL LEDGER   #201

Date	Item	Post. Ref.	Debit	Credit	Balance
May					

Notes

O'Malley, Capital   GENERAL LEDGER   #300

Date	Item	Post. Ref.	Debit	Credit	Balance
May					

Consulting Fees   GENERAL LEDGER   #400

Date	Item	Post. Ref.	Debit	Credit	Balance
May					

Rent Expense   GENERAL LEDGER   #500

Date	Item	Post. Ref.	Debit	Credit	Balance
May					

Telephone Expense   GENERAL LEDGER   #501

Date	Item	Post. Ref.	Debit	Credit	Balance
May					

Utility Expense   GENERAL LEDGER   #502

Date	Item	Post. Ref.	Debit	Credit	Balance
May					

Wages Expense   GENERAL LEDGER   #503

Date	Item	Post. Ref.	Debit	Credit	Balance
May					

Notes

Trial Balance	Debit	Credit
Cash		
Supplies		
Prepaid Insurance		
Accounts Payable		
Notes Payable		
O'Malley, Capital		
Consulting Fees		
Rent Expense		
Telephone Expense		
Utility Expense		
Wages Expense		
TOTALS		

(Do you balance? Debits should total $14,200 and credits should total $14,200.)

ADJUSTING ENTRIES:
The following adjustments are needed as of May 31:

(a)
$400 of the supplies were used.

(b)
$500 of the insurance has expired.

(c)
O'Malley determined that he has earned $2,000 in consulting fees for May for which he has not yet billed clients.

Work Sheet

Accounts	Trial Balance		Adjusting Entries		Adjusted Trial Balance		Balance Sheet		Income Statement	
	Debit	Credit	Debit	Credit	Debit	Credit	Debit	Credit	Debit	Credit
Cash										
Supplies										
Prepaid Insurance										
Accounts Payable										
Notes Payable										
O'Malley, Capital										
Consulting Fees										
Rent Expense										
Telephone Expense										
Utility Expense										
Wages Expense										

Notes